D1594006

Distributed in the British Commonwealth (excluding Canada and the Far East) by Ward Lock & Company Ltd., London and Sydney; in Continental Europe by Boxerbooks, Inc., Zurich; and in the Far East by Japan Publications Trading Co., C.P.O. Box 722, Tokyo. Published by Kodansha International Ltd., 2-12-21, Otowa, Bunkyo-ku, Tokyo 112, Japan and Kodansha International/USA, Ltd., 599 College Avenue, Palo Alto, California 94306. Copyright in Japan, 1971, by Kodansha International Ltd. All rights reserved. Printed in Japan.

LCC 76-158637
ISBN 0-87011-152-3
JBC No. 0026-782995-2361

First edition, 1971

Contents

МОНГОЛЬСКОМУ НАРОДУ ПО СЛУЧАЮ 50-Й
ГОДОВШИНЫ МОНГОЛЬСКОЙ НАРОДНОЙ
РЕСПУБЛИКИ

To the Mongolian people on the fiftieth anniversary of
their republic.

ACKNOWLEDGMENTS

*The author wishes to thank Dr. Katsuhiko Tanaka of the Tokyo
University of Foreign Studies, who contributed many photographs
to this volume, and Elizabeth H. Rose, who helped prepare the
chronology.*

PHOTO CREDITS: *Dr. Katsuhiko Tanaka; Keystone Press;
Albert Axelbank*

Mongolia

Rebirth of a Nation

One day, as I stood on the sands of the Gobi Desert, the thought struck me that were I to travel southwest for a thousand miles I would still be within the confines of the Great Gobi. It was a sobering, indeed a staggering, reflection, and with it came a feeling of kinship with Marco Polo and the account of his storybook travels in the great empire of Kublai Khan some seven centuries ago.

A cold wind was rising, although a bright sun cast lukewarm rays out of the clear, cloudless, typically Mongolian sky—a sky that was wholly innocent of the grime and smoke that pollute so much of our twentieth-century world. Save for my rented jeep, there was not a single man-made object to be seen—not a single signboard extolling the pleasures of American soft drinks or the technological splendors of Japanese cameras. The world was empty and strange and enthralling. Standing there in the desert beside my jeep, I sensed a momentary obliviousness of time: a mystical identification with eternity.

Mongolia! I remember, when I was a child, rolling the word on my tongue, savoring the charm of its liquid sounds. Everything I knew about this strange, intriguing place had come out of books until, in the early 1960s, I found myself in Taiwan. There, as bureau chief for an American news agency, I actually met some Mongols. They were elderly men, between sixty and seventy most of them, but they seemed so healthy and vigorous as to be untouched by mortality. Pleasant, agreeable men, who spoke little and who appeared remarkably indifferent to my presence, they rekindled my old interest in their remote land. I was now determined to visit it.

But desire was a far cry from reality: going to Mongolia, I soon learned, was no light undertaking. I had moved from Taiwan to Tokyo, and there, during the course of the next six years, I wrote letters to the relevant government bureaus requesting a Mongolian visa—and for the next six years I received not a single reply. I decided that the Mongolian bureaucracy would probably win hands-down in a request-ignoring contest—despite the great skill other bureaucracies have shown in this popular art.

And then I had a stroke of luck. Attending an economic conclave in Tokyo, sponsored by the United Nations, was a high-ranking Mongol government official, and a colleague from the Soviet press who was working in the Japanese capital was kind enough to arrange an introduction for me. From broad hints that the Mongol official let fall, I gathered that he was going to help me get that tantalizing visa. And he must have—for in the course of time I got it.

(After I was in the country, I understood one of the reasons for the Mongols' extreme reluctance to grant visas: they feel that many visitors from both East and West have unfairly maligned their country. The nation's budding tourist industry has only recently developed to the point where it can cope, more or less effectively, with the sometimes extravagant demands of today's pampered travelers. Several of the top officials of the Mongol tourist agencies were studying English while I was in Ulan Bator. It is hardly surprising that the government should read with considerable care the illustrated articles and books that have been produced by foreign visitors to the country—and many of these the officials have deemed guilty of error or distortion.)

The official telegram I received approved my visit for the month of March, which I found somewhat dismaying, for March temperatures in Mongolia are normally well below freezing—sometimes as much as 50° F. below freezing after the sun goes down. For that reason, summer is the best time of year to tour Mongolia, although even the summer months can be chilly. Once I had received the telegram, however, I had no intention of asking for a postponement: I feared not only that I would not get it but also that the "invitation" might be withdrawn. In any case, I was so elated at the prospect of finally making that long-coveted trip, I knew I could not let a little frosty weather get in my way. To prepare for it, I ignored the hazards to life and limb and took up, for the first time, the ungentle art of skiing. I took a gondola up to the peak of Mount Zao, northeast of Tokyo, and skied down—although in this case the verb may be an overstatement. It might be more accurate to say I slipped, slid, and tumbled down Zao's stern, snowy face.

I now considered myself more or less ready for the rigors of Mongolia, although I realized I still had some shopping to do. I bought the heaviest woolen underwear I could find, some extra pairs of gloves, and a pair of waterproof boots. As it was, I regretted none of those purchases—Mongolia was three or four times colder than anything I had previously experienced; even at ten in the morning, with the sun high in the sky, my ears began to tingle with the

MONGOLIA ✃

freezing cold if I left them uncovered for a short while; and if I took off my two pairs of gloves, in order to work my cameras, my fingers became uselessly numb in a few seconds.

Landlocked Mongolia is bordered by China on the south and Russia on the north, and so the visitor to the country is obliged to travel across one of these two huge countries. While a few travelers to Mongolia come via Peking, most enter from Siberia—and the latter was the only entranceway available to me, since the Chinese have, with unrivaled persistence, refused to grant me a visa.

Relations between Mongolia and her two giant neighbors are a study in contrasts. Sino-Mongol contact is, like the climate, cool, with almost no trade, while Russo-Mongol ties are warm, with an annual two-way trade of some two hundred million dollars. Mongols and Chinese periodically accuse each other of bad manners and violations of the border; Mongols and Russians are not merely friendly, they intermarry.

Obviously, then, Mongolia is on Moscow's side in her scuffle with Peking. There are sound historical reasons for this intimacy between the Russians and the Mongols. On several occasions in the present century the two fought together against a common enemy. In the 1920s, Red Army men helped the Mongols defeat counter-revolutionary elements, and again in 1939, at Nomonhan (Khalkhin-Gol), the two combined to repel a strong Japanese invading force. Mongols also were of help to the Soviets in hurling back the Nazis. One must take note of the fact, however, that although the dominant influence in present-day Mongolia comes from Moscow, not Peking, the dominant note artistically is Chinese. The visitor to Ulan Bator, the capital, soon discovers that the buildings he admires most were put up by the Chinese.

10

My journey to Ulan Bator from Yokohama was made by ship, train, and plane. The brief sea voyage, which was extremely pleasant, was spent mostly in the company of Japanese, who were on their way to the Siberian mainland, which they would cross, some by train, some by plane, in order to get to Europe. So far as I know, I was the only passenger on the ship who was headed for Mongolia. In fact, I should not be surprised to learn that during my stay in Mongolia I was the only tourist in the whole country—which is roughly the size of Western Europe. I know for a fact that I was the only North American there, and I never spotted a single Japanese, who are among the most peripatetic of travelers.

Irkutsk is the gateway to Mongolia from the north. When I arrived, this Siberian city, which has an exciting frontier air to it, lay under a thick mantle of snow. Nearby, Lake Baikal, the deepest freshwater lake in the world, stretched out like an immense white-frosted cake with little black dots on it. The dots were trucks and cars crawling over the lake's frozen surface, using the thick ice as a smooth and spacious highway without speed limits.

I had two days to wait before catching the plane for Ulan Bator—two rather dull days, as it happened, for there was not a great deal to do in Irkutsk and its streets were deep in slush. I visited two old churches, with their onion-shaped domes, the large technological college (which has an enrollment of more than ten thousand students), and finally, in desperation, a language school, where I watched French, English, Spanish, and German being taught.

Strangely, acquiring my visa from the Mongol consulate took only three minutes. I had anticipated hours of red tape—of which, as it turned out, there was none. My spirits were shaken, however, when Intourist, the official Soviet government travel agency,

MONGOLIA ☒

solemnly told me that there might not be a seat available on the plane to Ulan Bator. That would mean a wait of another three days.

But Intourist was unduly pessimistic. When I finally boarded the twin-engine Mongol Air Lines plane (Soviet built, of course), I found that there were only four other passengers occupying the fifty-odd seats: three Bulgarians and a Mongol, the latter in military uniform.

The flight from Irkutsk to Ulan Bator is less than two hours, and within thirty minutes of departure we were over Mongolia. Below I saw a couple of icy rivers winding among rounded hills of a pleasing light brown color. Although we flew quite low, almost (it felt) as though we were skimming over the tops of the trees, there were no houses to be seen, nor any visible signs of humanity.

Soon the stewardess served us tea Mongolian style—which means it had butter in it instead of milk or cream. Although this sounds like an outlandish idea, the tea is actually quite tasty once you become accustomed to the novelty. The girl who served us was tall and amply built, and I noted with interest that she had made liberal use of cosmetics. I concluded, therefore, that she was more akin to her Japanese and Western sisters than to the girls of China. The latter, addicted to unbecoming caps and baggy pants, religiously forgo powder and lipstick and mascara. Because of the priority given to "affairs of state," femininity (at least, as we think of it) has—so I am told—all but disappeared from the Chinese scene. I hoped the same would not turn out to be true of Mongolia—and I took our maquillaged stewardess to be a good omen.

I looked down; we were now flying so low I could make out a highway and a single-track railway beneath us, and within a few minutes we were touching down at the airport of Ulan Bator. I noticed a few olive-colored, single-propeller planes as well as several helicopters parked on the landing field. The surrounding scene was superb: low hills, covered in snow, glistening in the soft, cheerful light of the Mongolian sun.

I looked around, trusting there would be someone from the government to meet me; otherwise, I had been warned, I might have great difficulty negotiating a ride into the city, which is about fifteen miles away. So, before sailing from Yokohama, I had cabled my arrival date to both the Foreign Ministry and Julchin, the official travel bureau. I had done the same, on the previous day, at Irkutsk. Alas, although I tried to look as hopeful as possible, nobody appeared to be expecting me or to have the slightest interest in my presence. (Later I learned that neither telegram I sent had arrived— but would the following day.) There was not a sign of a bus or a taxi at the airport.

I began to feel rather like a guest at a party who has been invited by mistake; it is not a comforting feeling. Then a young, uniformed guard approached me. Although I do not think he knew more than thirty words of English, we succeeded in communicating splendidly. My unfortunate plight got through to him, and he helpfully placed some phone calls to the capital. As a result, a black Volga car arrived within an hour to take me to my hotel. Customs was easy, after I signed a statement in both Russian and Mongolian declaring that I had no guns or other dangerous implements with me, and we were soon following the long, winding road to the capital.

I felt like an invited guest again—but one who had come to the party under rather unusual circumstances, for I had in my pocket only the remains of a one-way ticket. Generally socialist countries insist, with unyielding tenacity, that the foreign visitor come armed with a ticket out. Despite this rigid rule, however, I had been sold a one-way passage from Yokohama to Ulan Bator (a distance of nearly four thousand miles, incidentally, for which I paid about two hundred dollars). One reason I was pleased to be in Mongolia without a ticket out or a fixed date of departure was that I did not know how long I would want to stay in the country. At least one month. Perhaps two? Perhaps even longer if the Mongols would permit it.

Accompanying me on the way from the airport to the city were two young Mongol men, who kept plying me with questions about my trip as well as about America and Japan. Only half listening, I am afraid I gave very brief and unsatisfactory replies. Some people go from one strange country to another and expend as little mental and emotional effort as though they were merely taking a commuter train from a suburb to a nearby city. Myself, I need more time to adjust, to calm down. And when, beside the road, we passed some *yurts* (a type of Mongolian tent that resembles a giant mushroom), I could hardly restrain myself. I wanted to leap out of the car, where it seemed to me I was merely a spectator watching a film about Mongolia. I wanted to get into the picture myself. But I restrained my desire: I had as yet no idea how such impulsive action might strike my Mongol hosts.

Ulan Bator is a clean, very attractive little city with a population of about a quarter of a million. It looks rather like a watercolor done in pastel tones by a happy and wholly uninhibited artist. Of the major public buildings, one is yellow, another lavender, several are pale green, and others are orange or milky white. Here and there a building will have tall, white columns that give it a Greek look, while right next door is a structure with a white steeple, resembling a New England church.

My hotel, which was named for the city, was a gray stone building that had been put up by the Chinese and furnished—almost dazzlingly—by the Czechs. It has six floors, with over a hundred rooms and a fine dining hall whose high ceiling is supported by a dozen columns of pale green marble.

When needed, the dining hall is converted into a ballroom, and one Saturday night I attended a party there. It was a lively affair, with a bright, loud juke box blaring hit tunes by such eminent bourgeois artists as Frank Sinatra, Dean Martin, Petula Clark, Fats Waller, and Herb Alpert—in addition to some Russian and East European singers. Sitting with some people from the British embassy, I was suddenly tempted to dance with an extremely pretty Mongol lass who sat a few tables away. My impulse, I am glad to report, was not rebuffed—although the poor girl was so shy she never once looked at me all the while we danced.

Ulan Bator (which, by the way, means "Red Hero") manages to get along very nicely without a single real nightclub, bar, or cabaret and the accommodating ladies that always seem to be associated with such establishments. The city does, however, have a dozen movie theaters, which are usually packed. At the time I was there, crowds were lining up to see a Hollywood spectacle, a little

MONGOLIA ✂

trifle called *Spartacus*, which was (so I was told) the most popular movie to hit the capital of Mongolia in many a year. I wondered whether the fact that Spartacus led the revolt of the slaves against Rome had anything to do with the film's popularity.

Popular also are the Opera and Ballet Theater, the Folk Arts Theater, and some astonishingly good museums. One evening I went to a performance of *Three Sad Hills*, an opera written around 1935 by the late poet, D. Natsakdorji, who is often called the father of modern Mongolian literature. The plot is simplicity itself: a poor shepherdess, although she loves a young herdsman, is forced to marry a rich, nasty merchant prince; but the brave young herdsman, with the help of his friends, succeeds in rescuing his beloved. I was, quite unashamedly, enraptured by it. The performance itself was extremely professional, the voices were strong and clear, the music was enchanting, and some of the melodies were unforgettable. Contributing to my own excitement was the infectious excitement of the audience, many of whom were standing because the theater was so crowded. I succeeded, luckily, in recording most of the opera, so I may be one of the very few people outside Mongolia who can hear *Three Sad Hills* whenever I wish.

Nationalism and flag waving are happily almost absent from the Mongolian scene, and one way this blissful lack of chauvinism makes itself apparent is in the large number of foreign plays given regularly in Ulan Bator's theaters. Performances of Molière, Goldoni, Lope de Vega, Gogol, Chekhov, and Shakespeare (especially *Othello*) are all well attended. Maxim Gorky, incidentally, seems to be the most popular author in Mongolia: the bookstores that I visited were all heavily stocked with his works.

On Ulan Bator's main boulevard—called Peace Street—are a

number of new apartment buildings, most of them four stories high, and the national department store. Nearby are the State University, the Academy of Sciences, and the State Library; and the city boasts, as well, three hospitals, numerous primary and secondary schools, a textile mill, a truck repair plant, a large plant for processing dairy products, and one for meat packing. Building cranes are a familiar sight in Ulan Bator, for the government is making a strenuous effort to move the city's fifty thousand tent dwellers into new brick apartment buildings, with plumbing and central heating, before the end of this decade. Without doubt Ulan Bator's architectural showpieces are the twin twelve-story apartment buildings erected by the Chinese at a time when Sino-Mongol relations were still cordial: the buildings are visible proof of the high architectural skill of the Chinese.

Two modern curses that citizens of the capital are free of are traffic accidents and air pollution from the exhausts of thousands of motor vehicles. In Ulan Bator the automobile is a luxury—and in many ways a liability (a horse or a camel is far less likely to get stuck in a snowdrift), and few of the capital's residents own cars. They use bicycles, buses, or their own legs. Perhaps for that reason all the people seem outstandingly healthy. Certainly the city hospitals that I visited were far from overpopulated—and I wondered if this was the result of Ulan Bator's style of unluxurious living.

The Mongolian People's Republic (to give it its official name)

MONGOLIA

is in many ways unique—in more ways, perhaps, than most other countries. Here are some points that occurred to me as I wandered about eagerly and inquisitively:

Mongolia is a socialist-pastoral country (which sounds, offhand, like a contradiction in terms).

The Lamaist church is state supported.

Tents (called *yurts*) are still the popular form of dwelling.

The constitution bans chauvinism and superpatriotism.

Family names may be as short as Es and as long as Tsembalvanchikdorji.

The annual average temperature in twenty-four hours at Ulan Bator (elevation 4,357 feet) is near freezing.

While wandering in the Gobi Desert, even tourists have stumbled upon sixty-million-year-old dinosaur eggs.

On October 23, 1970, the official Soviet news agency, Tass, reported from Ulan Bator: "The fossilized eggs of dinosaurs that disappeared 60 million years ago have been found by an expedition of Soviet and Mongolian scientists in the Gobi Desert. Dozens of egg deposits were found on the banks of a prehistoric river in the Gobi. The biggest deposit contained 16 such eggs. The dinosaurs were up to 100 feet long. The eggs found in the Gobi were about 10 inches in diameter."

Dinosaur eggs have never been on the menu of the Ulan Bator restaurant, but one has quite a wide choice there nonetheless:

oroomog, tsamba, arul, or *hoshnogo* for example. Curious? Well, the dishes are not so very odd, at least for anyone who has done a little traveling. *Oroomog* is sheep's intestine stuffed with liver and lights, while *tsamba* is merely roasted barley meal, and *arul* is dried cottage cheese. *Hoshnogo* is perhaps somewhat more unusual: the rectum of the sheep, turned inside out, stuffed, and stewed. Blood sausage is a common dish, and so are dishes made out of the roasted hooves and head of the sheep. The Mongols, it will be immediately apparent, are a thrifty people who dislike throwing things away.

Of course, for the less adventurous (like me), there is plenty of more ordinary food. I suffered no feeling of privation as I went through heaps of chicken, mutton, or beef, with rice, black bread and butter, stewed fruit, tea, fruit juice, or beer. Incidentally, both the *tsamba* and *arul* were delicious. (I must confess to having failed to sample the *hoshnogo* and the *oroomog.* Next trip, I hope.) And one day, in my honor, the hotel menu listed "Chicken a la Amerikanski" —it turned out to be southern fried chicken and was so good that I kept trying (to no avail) to order it again. Someone from the French embassy suggested that maybe the hotel had run out of chickens. (Prices, by the way, were not high; I rarely spent more than five dollars for a full-course meal.)

All the meat consumed in Mongolia is produced locally, although the rice and stewed fruit are imported, mostly from China and North Korea. Some of the rice comes all the way from North Vietnam. On occasion there is fresh fish from the nearby Tula River, and canned fish is imported from the Soviet Union.

Mongols are among the most aggressively hospitable people in the world and are forever offering food and drink to the stranger. Indeed, according to one of their ancient proverbs, no open-hearted

MONGOLIA ✖

visitor is considered to be a stranger. And if you do any traveling through the countryside, that will be the impression that you carry away. When you come upon a *yurt* pitched in the Great Gobi, the chances are strong that you will be asked to step inside, where you will be offered a cool drink and a place to relax. The drink will probably not be beer but rather *kumiss*—fermented mare's milk—which is said to be the reason Mongolians consider a longevity of three score and ten mere child's play. They opt for at least a hundred. And in more remote places I found that even an empty *yurt*, left unattended by its occupants, still offers refreshment. My guide explained that when *yurt* dwellers must be away for some time, they will frequently put food on the table, and any passerby is welcome to sit down and enjoy a bite—on the tent, so to speak.

Yurts constitute a familiar and very appealing feature of the Mongolian countryside. Of the two types of tent commonly used by the Mongols, one is of very simple construction and is intended solely for traveling. The *yurt* is a more permanent tent, although it too is portable; when the owner decides to change localities, he packs his *yurt* onto the backs of a couple of camels or horses—and off he goes, accompanied by his home. A round lattice framework covered by felt, the *yurt* from a distance, as already noted, looks like a monstrous mushroom. The Mongols claim that round houses are easier to keep warm in subfreezing temperatures than square or rectangular houses—and the Mongols ought to know.

Inside, the wooden support braces are painted in bright colors or patterns, and *yurts* nowadays sport many modern conveniences, such as electric lights and radios. Unlike his father, who probably slept on a very coarse mat, the present-day herdsman may retire for the night onto a soft, innerspring mattress. Outside some *yurts* one may see tethered not an angry camel but a scarlet motorcycle.

I had many questions I wanted to find the answers to during my short stay in Mongolia, and yet I realized from the start that I would probably understand very little unless I delved into the more recent history of the country—not the windswept Mongolian plain of Genghis Khan but the country around the turn of the century and in the years since.

The moment I began investigating, I discovered how appalled early twentieth-century travelers were by the misery and backwardness of the country. A Frenchman who visited Mongolia some fifty-five years ago made this fairly sweeping statement: "Conditions here are so wretched that it will need ten centuries for Mongolia to catch up with the rest of the world." Happily, recent events have proved him wrong, but at the dawn of the twentieth century Mongolia was still dragging both feet in the Middle Ages.

Few people were unaffected by disease, of which the venereal varieties were rampant. Less than two percent of the population could read and write. Dr. Sodnam Bira, a kindly gentleman of about sixty who is now attached to the Academy of Sciences, in telling me about his early childhood, said that nine of his thirteen brothers and sisters perished as the result of various childhood diseases. Medicine was an unknown luxury in Mongolia.

Another heavy yoke that the Mongols had to bear was the unreformed Lamaist church—whose priests accounted for perhaps half the male population. Poor, semiliterate at best, disease-ridden, committed to celibacy, these Lamaist priests were, in the opinion of many, a prime cause of Mongolia's economic stagnation. The result of this unfortunate situation was that for many people begging, prostitution, and theft frequently constituted the only means available for even minimal survival—until early death brought relief, frequently at under thirty years of age.

Today Mongolia, which has been a member of the United Nations since 1961, is a developing country that has already begun to outdistance various other nations of Africa, Asia, and Latin America. For the first time, Mongolia now produces enough wheat to fill all her domestic needs—and has a little left over for export. Nearly all her citizens are literate. And a baby born to a Mongol family today has a life expectancy of sixty-six years—as compared with about thirty half a century ago.

On the yardstick of international affluence, Mongolia remains, of course, a poor country. But the poverty is no longer the hopeless, grinding variety that it used to be. There are government programs for the building of schools and hospitals and for the welfare of the sick and the aged.

At the same time, the country is even striving to take its place among the more highly industrialized nations of the world. Walk down the streets of the capital, Ulan Bator, or of some of the other cities of Mongolia, and you will see dozens of Russians, both civilians and soldiers. The civilians, you will soon learn, are mostly technicians who are helping to build the factories that are an integral part of the government's five-year plans, while the soldiers are attached to work battalions. East Europeans, too, are helping Mongolia in her struggle to industrialize.

Because Mongolia has accepted, and is continuing to accept, all this aid from Russia and Russian satellites, she has been accused of being a "puppet" of Moscow. But such an accusation seems a bit exaggerated, given the miniscule population of the country (only a little more than one million), the extreme hardships suffered by her people, and the fact that until only a few years ago she was forced to channel all her energies into military purposes. Almost from the time of the 1921 Revolution right up to the formation of People's China in 1949, Mongolia's frontiers were in bitter dispute. When a poor country with a small population finds its borders threatened, virtually all that country's resources go into defense and everything else (including the economy) suffers.

I think that Premier Yumzhagin Tsedenbal's reply to critics who castigate Mongolia for leaning too heavily on Soviet aid is worth quoting. "If one has the power to carry only seventy kilograms," Tsedenbal said, "but wishes to carry 120 kilograms, then one carries his maximum seventy and asks others to help carry the remaining fifty. By doing that, it becomes possible to carry more in the same amount of time. Hence, it is possible to save time."

When we come to consider the Mongols in any historical context, we must bear in mind that many scholars believe them to have been the ancestors of a number of Oriental peoples. Mongol tribes are even thought to have migrated to Japan thousands of years ago. Indeed, many of the Mongol children that I saw bore an unques-

MONGOLIA ✋

tioned resemblance to those of Japan; and when I came back and
showed pictures of these Mongol children to Japanese friends, their
first remark was almost always, "Why, they look Japanese!"

The Mongols are divided into a number of so-called national-
ities; an official atlas lists fifteen of them, including Khalkas,
Kazaks, Buryats, Durbets, Bayats, Torgots, Darigangas, Uryankhas,
Mingans, Zakchins, Turks, Tuvins, Uzbeks, Hotons, Chinese, and
even a few Russians. They differ but slightly in dialect and customs, and there is no "interracial" strife reported among them.
By far the largest single group is the Khalkas, who compose some
seventy-five percent of the population and who inhabit a large
area of Mongolia, from the eastern borders to the Altai Mountains
and Lake Hubsugal in the northwest.

The turbulent history of the Mongols stretches back some ten
thousand years, to a time when nomadic tribes first peopled what
is now the territory of Mongolia. Recorded history comes later,
of course, with the incursions of the Huns and other nomads who
form the roots of the Mongol genealogical tree. The Hun Empire
stretched, in the third century A.D., from China's great wall in the
south to Lake Baikal in the north. Under Attila, the Huns pushed
towards Iran and the outposts of the Roman Empire, and in the
fourth and fifth centuries they invaded Italy itself. Peace to them
was only a stagnant, boring interval between wars. In the Noin-
Ula mountains of northwest Mongolia, tombs of Hun nobles have
been excavated and artifacts from many other lands have been discovered—lacquer bowls from China, for instance, and wool fabrics
from Greece.

It was around this time—in the sixth century—that the Mongols
adopted the ancient Aramaic script, which they continued to use

for over a thousand years until the introduction of the Cyrillic, or Russian, alphabet. At around the same time, the various tribes were confronted with a primitive kind of Buddhism.

But of more immediate import, in those turbulent days, were the rise and fall of empires, one succeeding another with bloodshed and shouting, until the dramatic appearance of Genghis Khan on the Mongolian stage. In the year 1206, having subjugated a number of Mongol tribes, he was proclaimed supreme ruler of Mongolia. His own name—Temujin—was discarded and he was given the title of Genghis Khan (or, as it might less familiarly but more accurately be spelled, Jinghiz Khan)—"Most Mighty King."

The present-day official view is that Genghis Khan's unification of the tribes was a boon to the land, while his military campaigns, including invasions of China, southern Caucasia, southern Russia, and the Persian Gulf, brought only devastation and misery to the conquered lands and peoples. Mongolia herself suffered both culturally and economically, and her people were dispersed over a large part of the sprawling empire. Thus, the country's own development was seriously retarded by its Most Mighty King.

His grandson, Kublai Khan, became emperor of China in 1271 and founded the Yüan dynasty. Under his rule, the Mongol Empire embraced Indochina, Tibet, the Persian Gulf, and the Black Sea. The capital was shifted from Karakorum (founded in 1227 A.D.) to the site of what is now Peking.

Then, following an all too familiar pattern, came internal rivalry and court intrigue; the constant warfare that ensued led to the decay of the empire and its eventual fall. After the Manchus had subjugated Mongolia, it remained within Manchu hegemony until 1911. Isolated from the rest of the world, the people were

MONGOLIA ✿

under the autocratic rule of Lamaist god-kings. No fresh breeze from the outside world touched the cloistered land.

Finally, on December 1, 1911, Mongol insurgents proclaimed their independence in a genuinely courageous document that said: "Our Mongolia, when first founded, was an independent country. According to this age-old right, therefore, Mongolia declares herself an independent state that will establish a new government and deal with the country's own affairs in which no other authorities may interfere. In keeping with this decision, we Mongolians declare ourselves from now on outside the jurisdiction of Manchu or Han officials. They have lost their power. They should leave our country and return to theirs at once."

Clearly a new Mongolia was in the making—but equally clearly the path was not going to be a smooth one. In 1915 czarist Russia signed a pact with China that recognized Mongolian autonomy—but within China. After the Bolsheviks came to power in 1917, this pact was discarded .

But Mongolia's troubles were by no means over. In 1919, thousands of Chinese troops invaded the country, and her so-called autonomy vanished. At the same time there entered upon the Mongolian stage one of the strangest characters it had ever seen, stranger even than any of the bloodthirsty Mongol conquerors: this was a White Russian named Roman Nicolas von Ungern-Sternberg, known as the Mad Baron. He had fought in the Russo-Japanese War of 1904–5 and was a member of the guard of the czarist diplomatic mission in Urga (the Mongol capital, which later became Ulan Bator). His grand plan now was, first, to restore the monarchies in Russia, China, and Mongolia; and second, and by no means less important, to establish a mammoth Central Asian state under the banner of imperial Japan. To set about this grand plan, he invaded Mongolia from the east with about a thousand troops.

Driven by a pathological hatred of Chinese and Red Russians, the Mad Baron spearheaded a reign of terror in Mongolia. Then, in a vast and pompous ceremony, he had himself anointed as the reincarnation of the Living Buddha—as the ruler of Mongolia was then called. People who were present at this glittering spectacle reported later that Ungern-Sternberg actually shed tears of emotion as he assumed the mantle of the Living Buddha.

Happily for the country, his end was not long in coming. In the summer of 1921, he was captured by Mongol and Red Army soldiers, stood up against a wall, and shot. The only tears known to have been shed on this occasion were those of joy.

Then, on July 11, 1921, Mongolian independence was once again proclaimed. This struggle for independence produced a few authentic heroes, two of whom—Sukhe Bator and Choibalsan—now share the same mausoleum, which is reminiscent of Lenin's tomb in Red Square and which also stands in the main plaza of the capital of the country. Sukhe Bator is immortalized as well by a statue that becomes a landmark to anyone who visits Ulan Bator.

The two men jointly formed the Mongolian People's Revolutionary Party (the name it bears to this day), but Sukhe Bator was the chief hero of Mongolia's struggle for independence. The son of a poor herdsman, he knew extreme hardship and privation as a child; growing up, he held various odd jobs, finally landing in the army. There, before the Bolshevik Revolution, he served under czarist instructors, displaying valor in combat and demonstrating qualities of leadership. (His name means "Axe Hero.") After the 1917 revolution, he fell under the Communist spell—for, as a Mongol proverb humorously puts states, "Ideas travel without visas."

Risking death if caught, Sukhe Bator crossed the Soviet border and made his way to Moscow, where he met Lenin, cementing future ties between the two countries. At the Mongols' First Party Congress, which met at a Soviet frontier town on March 1, 1921, friendship between the two countries was stressed, and a program was laid down that put basic reliance on the Soviet Union as a "necessary condition for Mongolia's liberation." Assisted by Red Army forces, Red Mongols captured their capital city in early July, 1921, thus eventually dooming the counterrevolutionaries, although armed struggles persisted for several more years.

Sukhe Bator himself died at the tragically young age of thirty. The official version at the time was that he had been poisoned by the Lamaist physicians who attended him, but a recently published official biography that I bought in Ulan Bator makes no mention of this supposed poisoning. The likeliest hypothesis is that the young revolutionary, the Axe Hero, was in fact suffering from tuberculosis but was too proudly stubborn to admit, even to himself, that he was ill. During Mongolia's terrible winter cold he insisted on making a tour of inspection of military garrisons—and a few days later, in his thirtieth year, he was dead.

I have mentioned Lamaism several times. Chiefly, I was curious to know how it was faring in the new, emerging People's Republic, and one bright, clear morning I set out to see if I could find the answer. I accompanied some Pakistani diplomats on a visit to Gandan Lamasery, which is located in the heart of Ulan Bator, about a five-minute ride from the hotel. Gandan is the only sanctuary in Mongolia where Lamaism still functions; other lavish temples have been transformed into museums.

We parked outside the high wall that surrounds the lamasery and entered through the main gate, passing a pair of stone animals with ferocious faces. Inside, two old men, wearing typical Mongol clothes, were prostrated on the ground, lying on wooden prayer boards. As we wandered from building to building inside the lamasery, we attracted a group of small children, who gaped at us, wide-eyed, while we snapped our cameras. I was much impressed by the tremendous disparity in age between the little children who followed us about and the old men lost in their devotions.

We were taken into the main temple by the chief abbot, a pleasant, serious, unsmiling man of about fifty. There the air was thick with the heady, sour-sweet smell of incense, and about two dozen lamas, heads shaved close and wearing saffron robes, were seated in rows. When we entered, they began praying in unison, as though on cue. A couple of drums banged and an instrument that looked like a bamboo horn tooted away. Some of the praying lamas peered at us out of the corners of their eyes.

At first I felt like an intruder at some private and sacred rite—but then I reflected that perhaps the priests actually enjoyed the diversion of seeing visiting foreigners as they toured the temple precincts. And I wondered if perhaps our presence gave the serene looking lamas a sense of increased usefulness.

For surely the lamas must realize that their church is gradually undergoing its death throes. They seemed to me, as we watched them at Gandan, less like priests than like curators in a museum, giving visitors a glimpse into the past. This feeling was strengthened when I asked the abbot about how many present-day Mongolians are followers of Lamaism. He tactfully avoided a direct reply, contenting himself with the statement that Lamaism "fully supports" state socialism. Obviously, lacking government funds, the church could not survive.

After we left the sanctuary, we were led into the guest house, an enormous *yurt* about ten yards in diameter and as warm and comfortable as any brick building could hope to be. The floor was almost entirely covered by a thick, maroon carpet; there were tapestries hanging behind deep sofas, with little tables in front of them; there were electric lamps—and there was a television set.

We were treated royally. First we drank a series of hearty toasts to international harmony, then there came the feast: a great variety of dishes of venison, beef, and mutton, all of this followed by exceedingly tasty pastries. As we ate, an attendant thrice filled my glass with Mongolian vodka (called *arkhe*); another glass would have put me under the table.

Mongolia was once a strong citadel of Lamaism, which for a time ruled supreme there and lay like a "strangling incubus" on the people. European travelers who came to Mongolia at the beginning of the present century were almost unanimous in their scathing denunciation of it.

Historically, it may be said to have had within itself the growing seed of its own destruction. Part of Mahayana Buddhism, and marked by great ritual and hierarchy, Lamaism became a powerful force during the time of Kublai Khan and during the thirteenth and fourteenth centuries entered Mongolia. Then, after the fall of the Mongol Empire, Buddhism gave way to shamanism, with its primitive stress on the warding off of evil spirits.

It was towards the end of the sixteenth century that Lamaism began to grow rapidly. Being a less refined form of Buddhism, it acted (so many scholars say) as a kind of brake upon the social and intellectual growth of Mongolia. However, one must note also that several monumental works of a theological nature were translated into Mongolian after the seventeenth century—translated by the tedious process of passing from Sanskrit to Tibetan and then to Mongolian. One such work was the *Ganjur* (of over a hundred volumes), and another was the *Danjur* (more than two hundred volumes). They are still to be seen in woodblock editions, a copy of the *Ganjur* being preserved in the State Library at Ulan Bator.

Some Western scholars assert that Lamaism was a vital unifying force among the Mongolian people. Whatever the merit of this view, it is unquestionably true that the Manchus (who exercised tight control over Mongol affairs up until the early years of the present century) made use of Lamaism to help them maintain their control.

When the new government came into power, after the Revolution of 1921, one of its first problems was how to dispose of Mongolia's tens of thousands of priests and its more than one hundred lamaseries. After my visit to Gandan, I discussed this problem with Dr. Bira, the academician. Speaking in English, he said: "We first gave vocational training to the young lamas, and we opened many factories and cooperatives to provide jobs for them. Of course we closed down many lamaseries. Most of the young lamas were willing to join cooperatives and enroll in schools after we persuaded them. This was far from easy. We had to divert the priests' former religious life into entirely new channels."

MONGOLIA 🌼

Dr. Bira stressed the fact that the priests had never previously toiled with their hands. Inevitably, he said, certain of the upper clergy rebelled and even organized counterrevolutionary guerilla bands. In the process of putting down this movement, some lamaseries were damaged and some of the lamas slain.

To prevent any further mass influx of young Mongols back into the Lamaist priesthood, the government passed a law providing that no male could become a priest until he had completed eight years of compulsory education. Then, during those eight years, the students were indoctrinated with studies on the wickedness of Lamaism; at the end of their education, few of the young men had any enthusiasm to enter the priesthood.

It must be noted that the state constitution guarantees freedom of worship, ensuring equal rights to all citizens, regardless of religion, race, or sex. Thus, the Lamaist church continues to exist, although there are presently only about a hundred priests in the entire country. There are several reasons why the Lamaist church is permitted to go on. One is that it supports the socialist regime, and at the same time it offers a rebuttal to critics of Mongolia who claim that the country has forcibly eliminated all religious worship. Another fact is that Mongolia is a member of the World Buddhist Association, through which it maintains a kinship with other Asian nations of Buddhist heritage.

The crowning glories of a country, it has been said, are its schools and universities, its teachers and students. In this respect, Mongolia has come a long way since the turn of the century, when education was the prerogative of the elect—a tiny fraction of the population; and the country continues to strive to improve the quality of its educational system. The process is, of course, gradual, but much progress has been made.

In 1927 a People's University was established at Ulan Bator. It was housed in a one-story brick building that contained classrooms, offices, library, and laboratory. Accomodations were provided in a spacious *yurt* dormitory for the dozen or so students who matriculated. Of these, some were women, indicating that Mongolia was one of the first of the Asian nations to inaugurate coeducation.

A larger university was projected, but its founding was delayed by the war against the Nazis, during which most Mongol men and women were mobilized. Finally, in 1942, the Mongolian State University in Ulan Bator opened its doors to about a hundred students. Today, more than six thousand students are enrolled in it, including about two dozen foreign students.

It has ten faculties, including natural sciences, social sciences (law, history, and journalism), engineering, and languages (Russian, English, Chinese, French, and Italian). The English department has, so I was told, some two hundred students. One reason for this rather large number is that Britain maintains diplomatic ties with Mongolia, and also there appear to be increasing—if so far unofficial—contacts between Mongols and Americans.

In addition to the State Univeristy, there are medical, agricultural, and teachers' colleges as well as various technical schools. In all, there must now be some twenty-five thousand students of higher learning enrolled in Mongolia's various institutions.

MONGOLIA ❦

At present, seven years of secondary education are compulsory for all Mongolians. The schools, both primary and secondary, that I visited in Ulan Bator and in north Mongolia appear to be well equipped, with adequate laboratories and classrooms and a corps of teachers that is both dedicated and able. By the beginning of 1971, one out of every six Mongols was attending some educational institute. General schools boasted an enrollment of some two hundred twenty-six thousand students, a rise of forty-five percent over the figure for 1965; and thirty-two thousand children were enrolled in the country's kindergartens, an advance of thirty percent over 1965. All the hundreds of children I saw looked happy, well dressed and well scrubbed.

Traditionally in Mongolia a woman was less highly valued than a head of livestock: to lose a domestic animal was a misfortune, to lose a wife was not, for she was far easier (and less expensive) to replace. When one Mongol man met another, he did not ask, as we do, "How's the wife?" but rather, "What's the condition of your livestock?" A man measured his real wealth by the number of animals—horses, camels, sheep, and goats—that he possessed. Family matters were of less importance.

On first examination, this may be a way of thought that the Westerner finds rather shocking. But in the United States, as in other "advanced" countries of the world, there are still many people who treat their dogs and cats better than they do other human beings, and like them better.

For centuries, then, women in Mongolia were considered to be merely sexual objects and, incidentally, child bearers. When Lamaism was at the height of its power, young women were often ravished in the temples. In one of Ulan Bator's museums there is a large

1. *Aeroflot* and Mongol Air Lines link Ulan Bator with Moscow, Irkutsk, Peking, and Pyongyang, as well as with provincial capitals within Mongolia itself.

6. *The Bridge of Friendship*, built by the Chinese during the "cordial" period, is representative of the Chinese contribution toward making Ulan Bator one of the more charming cities of the world.

7. *The Soviet Union* contributed greatly to the building of the National Theater, which faces the capital's Sukhe Bator Square, and is often referred to as "the little Bolshoi."

8. *Twelve-story apartment houses* (built by the Chinese) are used as hotels for foreign technicians, Communist diplomats, and visiting dignitaries. Most new apartment buildings in Ulan Bator are only four stories.

10. *The relief* at base of Sukhe Bator ▶ monument depicts a victorious operation by Mongol partisans (most of them nomads) during the Revolution.

9. *A Soviet officer*, serving as adviser to Mongolian armed forces, turns his face from the camera as he crosses Ulan Bator's main square; at left is kiosk selling photographs of prominent Mongols.

11. *The well-paved street* in front of Ulan Bator's government office buildings; extreme winter cold frequently causes cracks in road surfaces.

12. *The national* flag flies atop the Khural, or People's Assembly Hall, by Sukhe Bator Square.

13. *Hotel Ulan Bator*, where most tourists stay, is a modern, six-story building with over one hundred rooms (including deluxe suites) and a spacious dining hall that becomes a ballroom on Saturday nights. A statue of Lenin fronts the hotel.

14. *Soviet-Mongol* relations were greatly strengthened during the time of Stalin, whose monumental statue stands in front of the Academy of Sciences building in Ulan Bator.

15. *The old and the new*: a woman and her grandson watching a pageant at a national anniversary in the capital.

16. *Children* outside a new housing development: the capital has many parks, playgrounds, and nurseries where working mothers may leave their children.

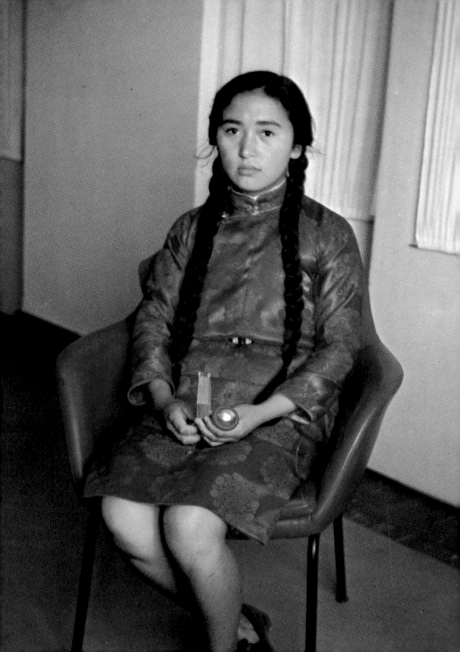

17-18. *Mongol women* have been "liberated" and enjoy equal rights with men, although many retain their traditional shyness in male company. The girl opposite works part time in the central post office, part time in a restaurant; below, a housewife at work in the wool spinning section of a textile factory in Ulan Bator.

19. *The show window* of a small, state-owned shop specializing in ,winter sports equipment; active sports are a passion with Mongols.

21. *A Mongol soldier* and one of the Chinese workers who helped in the building of the country stroll before the Univermag (state department store) display windows.

◄20. *Kiosks* sell all sorts of reading matter, including the official party newspaper, which has a circulation of over 100,000.

22. *The usual capacity crowd* watches a performance at the National Theater. Classic foreign plays are popular with Mongols, and way at the head of the list is Shakespeare's *Othello*.

23. *Singers* from western Mongolia, accompanied by native instruments, perform at the National Theater. On the curtain is the Soyombo, the national symbol.

24. *Mongol shoppers* can buy just about everything they need at the state department store (Univermag); some prices may seem high to the Westerner.

25. *The mausoleum* in Ulan Bator's main square is the last resting place of the country's two great heroes— Sukhe Bator and Choibalsan.

◄26. *Darkhan (preceding page)*, in northern Mongolia, not far from the Soviet border, is a new, rapidly growing industrial city, second only in size to the capital itself. Shown is a modern classroom in a Darkhan primary school.

62

27. *Young Pioneers* salute the author as he pauses in their classroom on a visit to one of Darkhan's extremely good schools. Some of the teachers are Russians.

28. *Midday calisthenics* occupy these primary school students in Darkhan, as a bust of Lenin smiles benignly.

29-31. *Schoolchildren* seem bright and cheerful while they sing and listen to an explanation from their music teacher.

32. *A proud youth* wears the red scarf that proves to the world he is a member of the Young Pioneers, an organization founded in 1925 to serve the country.

33. *An apple-cheeked girl* in Ulan Bator is all smiles; the state pampers its children—and their mothers too, awarding them the Order of Glorious Motherhood if they have five or more babies.

painting called the *Passion Buddha,* which depicts a nude holy man and a young girl in sexual congress, the lower halves of their bodies obscured by silk gauze.

Like most men in most countries of the world, Mongol men suffer a bit from the traditional masculine superiority complex. However, much progress in this respect has recently been made. Article 84 of the Constitution of 1960 provides that: "The infringement in any form whatever of the equal rights of men and women is forbidden by law."

In one textile factory I visited, the assistant manager was a woman, as were several engineers. The number of women doctors and teachers in the country is increasing notably, and of the fifty thousand members of the Mongolian People's Revolutionary Party twenty percent are women. To help safeguard the rights of the sex that is still considered weaker, there is the Council of Mongolian Women, which serves directly under the Council of Ministers.

The government is obviously—and justifiably—proud of the metamorphosis that has taken place in agriculture since the Revolution of 1921. For centuries Mongolia was a primitive land of stockbreeders who moved from place to place, driving their animals in search of forage, packing their tents and their other belongings onto their camels or horses. A few feudal lords owned about half of the country's livestock; the *arata* (herdsmen), who bore the brunt of

MONGOLIA ✌

taxation and other duties, lived uncertain lives. It has been estimated that in the year 1921 some two hundred thousand families were barely able to keep alive by husbanding animals on a small scale.

Of historic interest is the fact that the Mongols made the giant leap from ancient feudalism to twentieth-century state socialism without passing through the so-called transitional capitalist phase. By the 1960s, all the nation's herdsmen belonged to cooperatives or farm associations, and virtually all of the country's more than twenty-two million domestic animals were communally owned. The ancient, seemingly endless hand-to-mouth existence of the nomads had disappeared into the past.

Another revolution that has occurred in recent years is that Mongols have begun to work the soil. Men whose fathers were wandering sheep breeders now cultivate some eighty percent of the country's six million arable acres, raising apples, melons, beets, cabbage, wheat, rye, and barley. Russia provides tractors, grain harvesters, mobile generators, and other machinery; Mongolia, in return, sends the Russians such items as sheep guts and yak hair.

Still a third revolution that has taken place involves the Mongol worker. He is now employed in factories—which was altogether unheard of three or four decades ago. In the years immediately following the Revolution, all factory workers were imported from Russia, China, Germany, and elsewhere. Now—save for experts helping the nation build new plants and factories—all factory workers are Mongols, men and women both.

The result of all this economic ferment is that the average Mongol may now buy things he never dreamed possible: a pair of skis, a wristwatch, a camera, even a television set. All these consumer goods, and more, some of them imported, are available at the state department store called Univermag, a six-story emporium situated on the main boulevard of the capital. It is a Central Asian combination of Macy's and Selfridge's and Takashimaya.

Most of the goods sold at Univermag are, of course, the daily necessities of life: pots and pans, canned food, soap, rice, cloth, and so on. The prices did not seem to me exorbitant, although some items were certainly beyond the reach of the average Mongol. I noted down the cost of a few items, which I give here in their United States dollar equivalent:

Man's white shirt	$4.00
Woman's nylon blouse	$3.00
Woman's negligee	$2.75
Long cotton underwear	$4.50
High-heeled shoes (from Yugoslavia)	$28.00
Man's raincoat	$46.00
Man's heavy overcoat	$54.00
Woman's coat with fur collar	$75.00
Lamb's wool gloves (men or women)	$4.00
Skis (from USSR)	$14.00
Camera (Russian Zorki)	$150.00
Camera (Russian Pionyr)	$8.00
Film (black and white, USSR)	$2.50

There are, naturally, no idle rich in Mongolia, and workers are paid modest wages. Basic living costs, however, are exceptionally low: a two-room apartment in a state-owned apartment house, for example, rents for about $25 a month. Wages vary, of course. A herdsman receives about $70 a month, and a senior high school graduate draws much the same, while a university graduate will

get up to $120 a month. Factory workers are even better paid—
which would seem to indicate that Mongolia lays a higher price on
brawn than on brain.

The country's highest paid citizens are scholars, followed closely
by doctors, engineers, writers, and composers. They all earn over
$300 a month and in addition receive bonuses for creative work.
Bonuses are also paid to other workers who have been especially
zealous and efficient at their jobs, the sums ranging from twenty-
five to forty percent of their basic wage.

As for holidays and recreation, I was delighted to hear from my
guide, Dashjav Batur, that he spends two weeks every year at a
government-operated summer resort, which costs him about
$1.50 a day—including meals.

Mongolia's economic progress may be graphically illustrated by
a few important facts. The overall industrial growth rate, for example, is about ten percent, which is remarkable in a newly emerging
country. The government estimates that after two more five-year
plans have been accomplished—by 1980, that is—industry will
play a bigger role than agriculture in the national economy, in
terms of both emphasis and aggregate product. Mongolia, which
formerly had to import lumber, wool, linen, wheat, rye, barley, and
oats, is now self-sufficient in all these items. Of total Mongol ex-
ports, machinery and equipment jumped from twenty-two percent
in 1955 to more than fifty percent by the late 1960s, farm products
making up the remainder.

The other nations of the so-called communist bloc have of course
contributed generously to Mongolia's economic development,
chief among them being Russia and China. Then, in the early
1960s, China, taking ideological umbrage, bowed out, while Russia

has continued to offer a strong helping hand, as have the other nations of East Europe, the latter particularly in the field of technology. Since 1947, the Soviet Union has poured some two billion rubles' worth of loans, grants, and equipment into Mongolia; Peking's contribution, during the era of Sino-Mongol amity, amounted to about half that. As already noted, the foreigners one sees in Mongolia are mostly Russians or East Europeans, and they are mostly technicians helping with some industrial project.

I had heard glowing words of praise from so many Russians, as well as from the Mongols themselves, for the northern "miracle city" of Darkhan that I wanted very much to see it for myself. However, a visit turned out to be not at all easy, as few foreigners ever go to Darkhan, the chief reason apparently being that the tourist facilities there are considered inadequate. I announced, however, that I was fully prepared to sleep in a *yurt*—that, in fact, I wanted to do so very much. And so arrangements were, as they say, finalized.

At five o'clock in the morning on the day of the trip I went to the kitchen of the hotel, whose friendly cook had prepared, at my request, some provisions for the trip: hard-boiled eggs, cakes, and cider. We were three (an interpreter from the Foreign Ministry, a driver, and myself) and we had no trouble at all—during the four-hour journey—in doing away with the hotel's excellent provender.

Our vehicle was a competent Russian jeep, which took the winding, bumpy road in its stride. In places, the uneven road was covered with snow and ice, and sometimes, sitting in the back seat, I was knocked about so thoroughly that I began to feel groggy. Finally, I was able to brace myself somewhat by getting a tight grip on the overhead bar of the jeep.

Once we reached the outskirts of Darkhan (which means "Black-smith" in Mongol), we found ourselves driving on a splendid four-lane highway: an accomplishment of the new Mongolia. I could hardly believe my eyes, but my battered backside rejoiced.

We saw Russian soldiers working on the roads, while others were helping build new apartment houses. When I asked one of the soldiers if I could take his picture, he agreed, but before he posed for me, he took off his torn outer coat, brushed some dirt from his jacket, adjusted his cap to the proper angle, and put a red band around his upper arm. Then he stood smartly at attention for me. After I had taken his picture, I learned that he was twenty years old and came from the Siberian city of Irkutsk, just across the Mongol border. I promised to send a copy of the picture to his family.

In town I learned that I was not to sleep in a *yurt* after all but in a quite comfortably furnished apartment building of yellow brick. Our first stop was at a prefabricated hut used for conducting city business. There we met two men who were to be our companions for the next twenty-four hours: Suren Choinor and Echinkhorlo Gurrentsen. The former, who was thirty-seven years old, was an engineer; his wife, he told us, was a school teacher, and he had two young children, both of whom were enrolled in a state-run nursery. Our other companion was a journalist who wrote for the official Party organ, *Unen* ("Truth"). Both told us they were members of the People's Revolutionary Party.

The first thing we did, before undertaking anything so arduous as sightseeing, was to sit down to a splendid lunch—soup, followed by assorted meats and pickles, then canned fruit, and of course bread and *arkhe*, that potent Mongolian version of vodka. Inasmuch as the thermometer outside registered eleven degrees Fahrenheit, I decided the *arkhe* would be a safe precaution against the afternoon's sightseeing. The several cups of it that I drank did wonders for me.

All of Darkhan, I discovered, is divided in three parts: the industrial complex (a concentration of industry in the nearby valley), the old town, and the new town. All three parts are interconnected by means of pipes that conduct both steam heat and hot water. Ten years ago, Darkhan did not even appear on most official maps of Mongolia; today it is the second-ranking city in the country and figures prominently in the nation's industrial development. Its present population of thirty thousand is expected to double by 1980.

In the ten-square-mile valley (once known as "the Valley of God") that is adjacent to the city, I visited a brick factory, a cement plant, a thermal power station, a mechanized grain elevator, and a building-parts and materials plant. Under construction were a dairy and a plant for processing furs and skins. On the hills outside the city, which used to be bare (like many in Korea and China, where for centuries everybody cut trees down but nobody replaced them), thirty thousand poplars have been planted.

I wondered why Darkhan had been chosen to blossom industrially over the other towns of Mongolia and was told several reasons: nearby is the big Sharyngol open-pit coal mine, which, it is estimated, will not be exhausted for another half century; beneath the ground of Darkhan geologists have discovered untapped water resources; other raw materials available in the vicinity include both timber and iron; and, finally, Darkhan lies on the main north-south rail link between Irkutsk and Ulan Bator. The town is only a hundred miles from the Russian frontier.

Russian influence was evident at all the schools I visited in the course of an afternoon. Some of the teachers at the primary and secondary schools were Russians, and almost all the classrooms I visited had portraits of Lenin as well as of Sukhe Bator. In the First Secondary School I was shown a proud display of eight Mongol heroes, most of whom had died in the battle of Nomonhan in 1939, defending the nation against a strong Japanese invasion force. I gathered that learning about Mongolia's recent struggles is an integral part of every Mongol student's education.

That night one of my two new Darkhan friends said, "Do you want us to bring out the girls? Or would you rather see a film about the Mad Baron?" Reluctant to ask what "bringing out the girls" meant, I opted for the film—and tried to temper my regret at the choice I made by deciding that "bringing out the girls" meant no more than an evening of dancing. But I am still not sure.

A people's thinking is determined, in part certainly, by the use the government makes of the national language and by the extent to which both language and literature keep abreast of the times. It is noteworthy to see how Mongolia has fared in this regard.

One important event occured in 1941, when the ancient Mongol script vanished into history, a victim of what the twentieth century calls progress. It was in that year that the Mongols simplified and modernized their language and replaced their old alphabet with the Cyrillic, or Russian. Purven Horlo, the director of literature at the Academy of Sciences, was largely responsible for this laborious job of bringing the whole language up to date. In addition to adopting many foreign words, his department coined new ones where they were needed, thus greatly enriching the Mongol language. The newest dictionary contains over twenty-seven thousand definitions, while the standard two-volume Mongol-Russian dictionary (which Professor Horlo helped edit) has over fifty thousand entries.

Around this same period, the beginning of the 1940s, Mongolia's national literature began to flourish, while at the same time writers came to be aware of the close link that is forged in all Communist countries between state and artist. The state feeds and clothes the artist and in return expects him to conform to the ideals the state has laid down. (As seen in recent events in some socialist states, not all artists accept this relationship unmurmuringly.)

The Premier of Mongolia himself took up the cudgels in the late 1960s when he publicly regretted that too few works of Mongol literature today "reflect the inspired labor and heroic feats" of the country's revolutionary figures. He was referring, presumably, to the silent, unpublicized heroes and heroines among the ordinary people.

Premier Tsedenbal also suggested that it was up to the country's artists to raise their ideological level and skills constantly in order to "help mold future builders of socialism." To make certain that a "genuine creative spirit" prevails in all Mongolian art, Tsedenbal decreed that Party organs must increase their guidance over all art and literature. He proclaimed that the final responsibility of all artists is to the people.

Writers who have fallen under official displeasure are those, for instance, who have failed to criticize Genghis Khan, or who have written "too much" about religion, or who have neglected to place legend and history in stark contrast, or who have failed to make a revolutionary hero appear more heroic.

In the early 1940s, of course, anti-Nazi themes dominated most fiction, although older themes were also popular. Sengeh's short novel, *Ayushi*, tells of a courageous herdsman who led an uprising against Manchu feudal lords in 1903 and so initiated a movement toward independence. Sengeh, who studies at the Soviet Institute of Literature, has written a number of political poems, including "Red Square," "Lenin," and "Stalin." Others of his poems are dedicated to the furthering of friendly ties among all nations of the world.

Natsakdorji is frequently called "the father of modern literature" in Mongolia. In the early days of the republic he helped inaugurate a school of what has been described as "genuinely realist" literature. His short stories depict the life of working people after the Revolution, while many of his poems describe the lives of herdsmen. Here are a few lines from his most famous poem, "The Motherland," which has been set to music:

Khentei and Khangai, tall and majestic,
With their garment of forest, are the beauties of the North.
The deserts of Nomina and Sharga, with their boundless
  expanses

And sea of sand dunes, are the beauties of the South.
Such is my Mongolia, beloved forever.

When he died in 1937, Natsakdorji was only thirty-one years old.

Many young novelists have, of course, appeared during the postwar years. One is Chimido (born in 1926), whose novel *Spring and Fall* tells of young Mongols toiling in the Gobi Desert and of their tender feelings for each other. He has also written poems and critical articles, including a tract formidably entitled "Bourgeois Nationalist Ideological Influence on the Works of a Number of Mongolian Writers." Another well-known writer is Rinchin, who after the war published a celebrated trilogy called *Dawn*, which tells of the Mongol people's struggles for a freer and a happier life in the early years of the present century and which touches on events in China and Tibet as well as in Mongolia.

Playwriting too has flourished in the postwar era, and there are frequent productions of Natsakdorji's *Younger Generation* and of the plays of a woman dramatist named Oyun. Like many Mongol writers, Oyun studied in the Soviet Union and began her literary career by translating plays from Russian into Mongolian.

It must not, of course, be supposed that Mongol literature is confined to works of the twentieth century. Professor Purven Horlo expects to have completed, by the end of 1971, a textbook on Mongol folk literature, and he told me that, with the help of other scholars, he was also preparing a three-volume history of ancient Mongol literature.

One of the most moving documents in all Mongol literature is *The Secret History of the Mongols*, a prose-poem supposedly written around the middle of the thirteenth century. Depicting the barbarism of those bygone times, it has disturbing parallels with our own presumably more highly civilized age.

A short passage follows:

> The starry skies are overturned as people strain to smite each other;
> There is no peace on any pallet when all are striving after gain;
> Look at the whole wide world being split as people prepare for war!
> When, sword unsheathed, all rage together, who can lie down in peace?
> Can anybody escape from this plague of war?
> Who is aloof from this dreadful slaughter?

Of all Mongol sports, including archery and horseback riding, the most popular and the most highly regarded is wrestling. Every Mongol boy dreams of entering one of the big annual tournaments (the most important of which is held on Independence Day, July 11) and emerging first, thus earning the right to call himself an *arslan*, or "lion." The runner-up to an *arslan* is a *dzan*, an "elephant," while the man who places third is a *nachin*, or "eagle." Should someone be so skillful and so fortunate as to emerge victorious in a national tournament twice in a row, then he will have earned the title of *avrag*, "titan," the apex of Mongol wrestling, roughly equivalent to the "grand champion" rank in Japanese sumo.

৪ MONGOLIA

Among the Mongols, wrestling is a tradition that goes back hundreds of years, perhaps further back than recorded history. Chinese who visited Mongolia in the seventh century A.D. reported watching wrestling matches, and the chronicle of the Franciscan friar Carpini, who was in the Mongol capital of Karakorum in the thirteenth century, also mentions the sport.

The most illustrious of all Mongol wrestlers in the long history of the sport was Genghis Khan, who had the reputation of being the best wrestler in the land—a fact that may have aided him considerably in his assumption of absolute power. This agreeable picture of the great conqueror wrestling democratically with his soldiers is marred by stories of the great conqueror's extremely bad temper and treachery.

One story, for example, concerns his own younger brother and his wife's. The latter, whose name was Tebtengri, was—so the story goes—loud-mouthed and argumentative, and he had succeeded in humiliating Temugu (who was Genghis Khan's younger brother). There is a further suggestion that Genghis Khan suspected him also of seeking to usurp his own power. In any case, Genghis Khan slyly suggested that the two young men settle their differences by holding a wrestling match in the conqueror's own *yurt*.

The two wrestlers showed themselves to be equal in prowess, and the match was clearly a stalemate, when Genghis ordered them to go outside the *yurt* and continue the struggle to a more satisfactory conclusion. It was a prearranged trap. The moment Tebtengri stepped outside, he was seized by three wrestlers waiting there, who snapped his spine. After he was dead, the Great Khan is said to have remarked: "I cannot permit a man to live who would presumptuously seek to be my equal."

MONGOLIA

No doubt Genghis's action was by no means unique, for history tells us that in ancient times wrestlers fought so vigorously they frequently suffered broken bones. Such tactics have now been eliminated from the sport, and Mongol wrestling is perhaps the least brutal kind of body-contact sport practiced anywhere in the world. Kicking, punching, chopping, gouging, hair-pulling, and pinching are all disallowed—although brute strength is, of course, a most helpful asset.

Ages of the contestants vary greatly: they may be as young as eighteen or as old as forty-five. They are virtually naked, save for bikini-style trunks and a scanty shirt. The latter has short sleeves and no front, being joined by a length of material at the back, thus leaving the chest of the wrestler exposed. Colors are bright: red, green, yellow, even purple. Wrestlers who wear tiny peaked caps are the champions. Most have their hair cut short, but I saw one wrestler with long hair who was generously applauded by the audience—for his skill at wrestling, I assumed, not for his shining black tresses. Watching him fight, I thought how much he must resemble his medieval prototypes, when very likely everyone wore their hair long. Cheerful, sportsmanlike, and sturdy, he won the match—I am glad to say.

In recent years Mongolia has had crucial encounters with three of its neighbors—encounters that have shaped its modern history and greatly influenced its relations with the rest of the world.

One of the most critical of these encounters was the Battle of No-monhan, which occurred in the spring and summer of 1939, when the mighty Imperial Army of Japan was repulsed by joint Mongol and Russian forces. Nomonhan was a highly significant moment in modern history, for it was a major battle fought just before the outbreak of World War II and it constituted a defeat for Japan. Strangely enough, it has gone largely unreported.

As far back as 1935, the Japanese military had begun to probe the defenses of eastern Mongolia, obviously anticipating an invasion. The following year Japan joined Germany and Italy in what was called an anti-Comintern Pact, and by 1939 the "China Emergency" was already in its third year. By the hundreds of thousands, Japanese were making pilgrimages to Yasukuni Shrine in Tokyo to pray for the repose of souls of Japanese warriors killed in China. Early that same year the military decided to advance in strength into Mongolia.

No doubt to Japan the success of the invasion must have seemed a foregone conclusion. Mongolia itself was a hopelessly backward country, still living its feudal, nomadic life; while, to the Japanese, the Soviet Union seemed like a flabby giant far too preoccupied with her own internal problems (Stalin's ruthless purges were in full swing) to be able to fight a battle for Mongolia—despite the fact the Soviet Foreign Ministry had warned Japan that the Red Army would defend Mongolia's borders if Japan attacked.

Japan attacked, with a large force, using warplanes and tanks—and to the intense surprise and chagrin of the imperial war strategists the attack was repulsed. Side by side, Russian and Mongol warriors fought under the command of Marshal Grigori Zhukov (who later gained his chief fame fighting the Nazis). Then Zhukov counterattacked, and by the end of August he had driven the enemy off Mongol soil. It was a costly campaign for both sides: Japanese casualties, according to official Mongol records, came to nearly eighty thousand men killed and wounded, while Russians and Mongols suffered similarly heavy losses. By the Nomonhan River one may still see traces of trenches and dugouts, and at the top of Mount Zaison, on the outskirts of Ulan Bator, stands a white obelisk commemorating the thousands of Russian soldiers who lost their lives in the defense of Mongolia.

A truce was announced on September 16, 1939, and all fighting ceased. This truce had been signed, the Japanese Foreign Ministry insisted, solely for the purpose of settling a border dispute and would have no effect on the European situation. The latter had, obviously, undergone considerable changes since the Mongolian campaign was initiated: Russia and Germany had signed a non-aggression pact, and on September 1 Germany had invaded Poland. Despite the statements of the Foreign Ministry, however, some historians are of the opinion that it was the determined Soviet-Mongol resistance at Nomonhan that caused the Imperial Army to decide against war with Russia and to head, instead, further south.

Mongolia's relations with China have taken a far different course. For one thing, there is the undoubted fact that Chinese—or Han—culture is tremendously strong and tenacious. History has consistently shown that nations in touch with China have always fallen under her spell unless they have built strong walls against it. China's deep influence on Japan persists to this day, and Kublai Khan himself was far more influenced by China than China was by Kublai Khan. Dr. Owen Lattimore, the American authority on Mongolia, compares China to a camel that sticks its nose in your tent. Once you let it get its nose in, you will soon find the whole camel in your tent—and yourself on the outside.

In the early years of the present century, Chinese merchants in Mongolia were filling their pockets at the expense of the Mongols themselves. It has been estimated that there were seventy thousand Chinese merchants in the Mongol capital before independence; they were far and away the most numerous of foreign entrepreneurs.

More recently, official relations between China and Mongolia have had their ups and downs. The Kuomintang, fighting both the Japanese and the Communists, gave little heed to Mongolia's cry for independence until after the end of World War II. Then Generalissimo Chiang Kai-shek asked for a plebiscite, to which the Mongol government agreed.

Not a single vote was cast against independence in this 1945 plebiscite. The fact was confirmed by none other than Li Fa-chan, the Kuomintang's Vice-Minister of Internal Affairs, who was present in Mongolia as an observer. "The Mongols voted freely, voluntarily, and sincerely," Li affirmed.

He added: "This being the first time that my colleagues and I are here, Ulan Bator appears to us a modern city with many tall buildings, cultural institutions, and primary and middle schools. There are also a university, museums, and good theatres, and we have heard some good music." The Mongols, he said, were obviously capable of building their own country.

The Nationalist regime of China thus appeared to have given its recognition to independent Mongolia; it held off, however, on the exchange of diplomats, and later it reneged on the question of recognition. When, in October, 1949, the People's Republic of China was established, Mongolia promptly offered recognition,

MONGOLIA 🏵

and the following year diplomatic missions were exchanged between the two countries, missions that continue to exist today despite the cooling of Sino-Mongol relations since around 1960.

The Peking rulers, regarding themselves as Marxist purists, have accused the premier of Mongolia of being a "revisionist" and a "Titoist" and of causing "great losses" to the Mongolian economy. The Mongolian reaction has been a calm one. In 1969 a Foreign Ministry spokesman said: "There is no person in Mongolia who swallows such a false rumor as the one, coming over Chinese radio waves from Peking, that the Mongols' standard of living has been reduced to such an extent that six persons own a single suit of clothes jointly." This was such patent nonsense, the official said, that there was no need to jam Chinese radio waves.

That same year, 1969, the *People's Daily*, official organ of the Communist Party of China, charged that the Soviet Union had transformed Mongolia into a Russian colony. Inasmuch as Chinese influence in Mongolia had by that time virtually died, Peking was obviously probing for the Achilles' heel in Mongol-Soviet friendship, obviously hoping one day to woo Mongolia away from the Kremlin into the ample bosom of Mao.

All such attempts seem bound to fail.

The so-called cult of personality began and ended in Mongolia with one man—Marshal Choibalsan, Zhukov's colleague at the critical battle of Nomonhan, the leader of the Mongol forces who opposed the Japanese expeditionary army, a close friend of Sukhe Bator (Mongolia's great hero), and a revolutionary hero himself.

Born in 1895, Choibalsan was not quite thirty years old when, in 1924, he was appointed commander in chief of the Mongolian army upon the death of Sukhe Bator. He spoke fluent Russian, having studied military science in the Soviet Union. He became deputy premier in 1935 and, four years later, premier. It was then that he appears to have fallen under the influence of Josef Stalin; he even became known as Mongolia's little Stalin, and like big Stalin he unleashed some harsh purges in his country. He seems, however, to have had few opponents within his government.

One Mongolian poet, writing a tribute to Choibalsan on his fiftieth birthday, hailed him as "Stalin's pupil" and added: "Your heroic honor will inspire legends throughout the centuries. Live and work for us in good fortune! Live tens of centuries!"

Choibalsan died in 1952, a year before Stalin, and as soon as "de-Stalinization" set in, "de-Choibalsanization" followed. Yet it must be noted that, although Choibalsan may have built himself up into a kind of Mongol superman, he was never detested in his country, as Stalin came to be in his. (Strangely perhaps, Stalin is not hated in Mongolia: a monumental statue stands in front of the Academy of Sciences in Ulan Bator.) The State University boasts a statue of Choibalsan, and a city in eastern Mongolia has been named for him. Moreover, and more indicative perhaps, his remains lie alongside those of Sukhe Bator in a mausoleum on the capital plaza.

The present premier of Mongolia, who was born in 1916, is a good economist and is virtually self-effacing. Tsedenbal actually shuns publicity, and while I was in Mongolia I saw few copies of his portrait. He visits Moscow often, Peking less often, and has welcomed a number of world leaders to Ulan Bator, among them Marshal Tito of Yugoslavia. For his services to Russia during the war, Tsedenbal was twice awarded that nation's highest medal, Hero of the Soviet Union.

Inevitably Mongolia has failed in some of the giant strides she has been taking toward twentieth-century modernization, and Tsedenbal has himself pointed out some areas of low performance. He has criticized the "lax attitude" of party workers, as well as of some government agencies, in not pushing educational efforts vigorously enough.

The Mongolian People's Republic is harassed by problems common to all developing states. She still, for instance, lacks sufficient experienced managers and skilled workers. Some experts say that Mongols do not make the best use of their productive forces; often new equipment lies idle, building schedules may be postponed, new enterprises may be delayed, and warehouses are sometimes filled with an oversupply of raw materials or equipment waiting to be moved or installed.

Further education and training for Mongols and improved relations with more developed nations in both East and West will of course do much to remedy these defects. At the present time, Mongolia is striving for closer ties with the United States, Japan, and other world powers. Both Washington and Tokyo have announced that they are initiating "preliminary studies" of the recognition issue. One obstacle would appear to be the claim to Mongolian sovereignty by the Nationalist Chinese regime in Taiwan. However, Mr. U. Alexis Johnson, former American ambassador to Japan and now a top diplomat in the State Department, has told me that he sees no insuperable difficulties in the way of establishing better relations between the two countries. American and Mongol diplomats, to be sure, frequently rub elbows at diplomatic cocktail parties.

It seems almost safe, then, to look into the clouded crystal ball of world politics and predict that, in the not too distant future, relations between Washington and Ulan Bator are likely to expand and improve. One highly auspicious sign, surely, is that neither government prohibits visits by the other's nationals. All one needs is the urge to travel—and a visa.

Wisdom of Mongolia

(A Few Selected Proverbs)

- There is no better luck than being alive; there is no better science than experience.
- By gaining knowledge, you will understand your previous shortcomings.
- It is good if no cloud hides the sun; it is good if no laziness hampers the learner.
- No pains, no gains.
- Don't despair of knowledge being endless. Console yourself: you can only make small mistakes.
- Snow becomes whiter in the moonlight; wise men learn from wise words.
- Learning is the same as pocketing valuables.
- Difficulties educate, luxuries incapacitate.
- Distant mountains merge in mist and cloud; people far apart are united by deeds.
- An educated man is modest; a broad river is quiet.
- In the words of the old there is wisdom; in proverbs there are lessons.

- Don't be frightened by the unknown; don't hesitate to learn what is different.
- A dabbler in a good cause is like a bad portrait in a good frame.
- Trees are the beauty of a mountain; scholars are the ornaments of a state.
- Stars decorate the sky; broad knowledge enhances a man.
- The thoughts of a man are like the depths of the earth.
- In a poor *yurt*, too, scholars and poets are born.
- It is best to speak little and to think more.
- Only one light disperses night's darkness.
- A bad master has many tools but few brains.
- An ignorant man boasts of his knowledge.
- By the teacher you judge the students; by the students you judge the teacher.
- He can't add one and zero.
- What is done in haste is often waste.
- The keen will find; the careless will lose.
- His hands do not reach the saddle but he reaches for the sky.
- His talk is that of a wise man; his deeds are those of a fool.
- The harder the youth the easier the age.
- Laziness fattens.
- There is no bird that doesn't need wings; there is no man who doesn't need peace.
- A problem is better solved by peace than by fighting.
- Experience teaches caution.
- Even a wise man needs a friend; even a strong man needs help.
- An unreliable friend is worse than a fierce enemy.

MONGOLIA ✿

- Friendship eases hardship.
- When people fight, traitors delight.
- He who likes people has many friends.
- A reliable friend can replace even blood relatives.
- Though you have wits of your own, consult a friend.
- Once friends, friends forever.
- A good heart is better than an open mind.
- The stronger the friendship, the smaller the differences.
- You can't cover the sun with your palms.

34. *The ornamental gate* of Gandan Lamasery shows rich Chinese influence. Children play as the priests chant sutras, and tourists are welcomed; afterwards they are served a delicious meal in a *yurt* nearby.

35. *A Buddhist stupa* that is said to possess some of the bones of Gautama Buddha. The faithful prostrate themselves on the wooden boards in front.

36. *Mongolia's hundred thousand lamas* were reeducated after the turn of the century to do productive work; today there are only about one hundred lamas at Gandan, which receives a state subsidy.

37. *Elderly Mongols* gather at Gandan, waiting to be called to prayer. Often they pray for distant family members, attaching their names to prayer wheels outside the temple.

38. *An old-timer* (*preceding page*), near Gandan Lamasery, makes use of Mongolia's surest and most familiar means of transport. Except for confirmed city dwellers, every Mongol owns his own horse.

39. *The large yurt* used to entertain visitors at Gandan is full of modern conveniences, including a television set. A carpet more than twenty feet square covers most of the floor space.

40. *Lamaist priests*, supported by the Marxist Mongolian state, say they favor "peace and socialism" and pray for the brotherhood of man.

41. *Monasteries (preceding page)* are museums today and are visited mainly by foreign tourists; Mongols themselves have little to do with the surviving relics of Lamaism. Some modern-day scholars blame the once powerful lamas for the poverty and backwardness of the people before the Revolution.

42-43. *National Day* (July 11) commemorates the establishment of the Mongolian People's Republic. The traditional symbolic color is blue, which dates back to the time of Genghis Khan; red, of course, stands for the Revolution.

44-46. *Sports* are one of the chief features of the National Day celebrations, and the most popular of all Mongolian sports is wrestling. In former days, contests frequently ended in death; now they follow rules the Marquis of Queensbury would approve. Champion wrestlers are among the most celebrated figures in today's Mongolia, and every little boy hopes some day to become an *arslan*, a lion.

47. *Chinese parasols* shade this Mongol family as they relax at a commune outside Ulan Bator during an archery festival. The metal jug in the foreground is filled with fermented mare's milk (*kumiss*), which is very popular with Mongols but which may leave the visitor with a mild hangover.

48-49. *The winner of a horse race* has just received his prize—a bowl of *kumiss*. He pours some over the horse's mane first, then drains the bowl himself. The winner in the race will be presented to the premier.

50-51. *Archery* is a popular sport for both men and women, and contests are part of National Day celebrations.

52. *The brand mark* (*overleaf*) on a ▶ horse's flank identifies the animal for its owner; there are very few fences in Mongolia.

Chronology

8000 B.C.   Nomadic peoples inhabit Mongolian steppes.

300 B.C.   Hun Empire founded on present Mongolian territory; included Mongol and Turkish tribes.

100 B.C.   Hun Empire splits: southern tribes accept Chinese authority; northern tribes under Attila advance to borders of Roman Empire.

500 A.D.   Powerful Turkish kingdoms appear successively. Buddhism and Christianity become widespread. Script taken from ancient Aramaic adopted; in use until 1941.

1000   Kidan Empire established on present Mongol territory and in northern China. Lasted 200 years.

1200   Present territory of Mongolia peopled by many tribes with no unified rule.

1206   Genghis Khan unifies tribes. Begins conquest of China, Central Asia, southern Russia, Persian Gulf.

1227   Death of Genghis Khan. His son Ogotai becomes new khan. Mongol capital of Karakorum founded, becoming hub of gigantic empire. Russia, Poland, and Hungary invaded.

1246   First European envoys report on splendor of Kara-korum, its palaces, artisans, actors, doctors, mathe-maticans—many of European origin.

1251   Emissary from King Louis IX of France sees Buddhist temples, Christian churches, and two Moslem mosques at Karakorum.

1258   Mongols capture and sack Baghdad; destroy 4,000-year-old irrigation system.

1259–94 Kublai Khan moves capital to Yenking (Peking). Founds Yüan, or Mongol, dynasty, including part of Indochina and Tibet. Frontiers stretch to Persian Gulf and Black Sea.

1200s   Writing of the *Secret History of the Mongols* started.

1260   Sultan of Egypt defeats Mongol army.

1271–95 Marco Polo visits China of Kublai Khan.

1274   Mongols make first unsuccessful invasion of Japan.

1281   Mongols' second attempt to invade Japan ends in disaster.

1368   End of Yüan dynasty. Mongol Empire begins to crumble. Karakorum razed.

1400   Mongolia broken up into disunited areas.

1649   Urga—the present Ulan Bator—founded.

1691–1911	Manchus conquer Mongolia. Mongols reduced to serfdom and poverty for over 200 years.
1911	Mongolia declares herself independent state. An uprising of herdsmen becomes a revolutionary movement against Ch'ing dynasty.
1915	Russia, China and Mongolia sign an agreement defining Mongolia's international position.
1919	Mongolia is forced to surrender its autonomy. Chinese military dictatorship established.
1920	White Guards of "Mad Baron" Ungern-Sternberg invade Mongolia. Revolution erupts. Mongolian People's Revolutionary Party formed.
1921	Revolutionary regime requests presence of Soviet Red Army units inside Mongolia. New law liberates 100,000 herdsmen from serfdom. Debts to foreigners canceled. July 11: People's government formed, under a temporary, limited monarchy. November 5: Treaty of Friendship signed with Soviet Union.
1922	Remnants of White Guards defeated.
1923	Hereditary rights of feudal lords abolished. First industrial enterprises set up to improve animal husbandry. Consumer cooperatives formed.
1924	Industrial and Commercial Bank created to control currency. Death of Bogda Khan ends limited monarchy.
1936	Mutual assistance pact signed with U.S.S.R.

MONGOLIA ✆

1939	Japan launches attack against Mongolia at Nomonhan; Japan defeated by Soviet-Mongol armies.
1941	Nazi Germany invades Russia. Mongolia declares its assistance.
1945	Mongol armies help liberate northeast China and Inner Mongolia.
1946	Kuomintang government of China recognizes Mongolia as an independent state after plebiscite, but later withdraws recognition.
1947	First Five-Year Plan adopted.
1956	Economic assistance pact with Peking signed.
1959	Sino-Soviet treaty guarantees independence of Mongolia.
1960	New constitution adopted.
1961	Mongolia enters United Nations.
1962	Border agreement signed with Peking.
1963	Britain establishes diplomatic ties with Mongolia.
1966	France establishes diplomatic ties with Mongolia.
1969	May 23: Mongolia invited to be member of Geneva Disarmament Conference.
1970	Italy establishes diplomatic ties with Mongolia.

Suggested Reading

C. R. Bawden. *Modern History of Mongolia*. London, 1969

Owen Lattimore. *Nomads and Commissars*. New York, 1956

A. J. K. Sanders. *The People's Republic of Mongolia* (General Reference Guide). London, 1968

Robert Rupen. *Mongolian People's Republic*. Stanford, 1966

S. Sandag. *Mongolian People's Struggle for National Independence and the Building of a New Life*. Ulan Bator, 1966

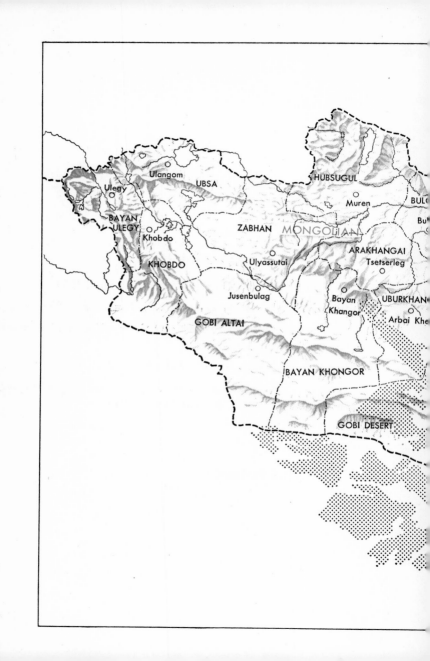

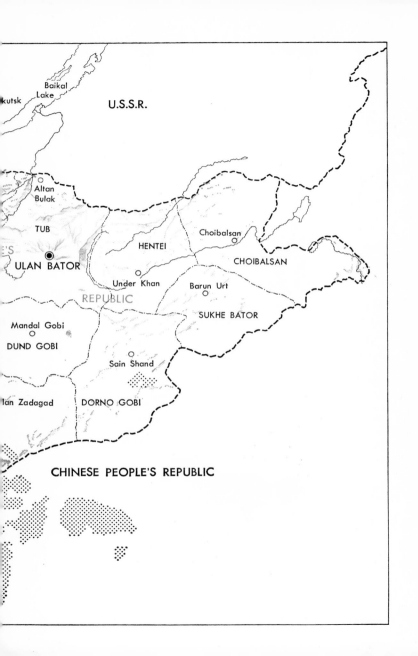

54. *Cars* (*overleaf*) may run out of ▶ fuel, the Mongols say, or get stuck in the snow, but as long as you feed your horse you will never lack transportation. All Mongols are good horsemen, and many ride bareback.

53. *Soldiers* who gave their lives in Mongolia's twentieth-century struggles make up an impressive lesson for the children of the First Secondary School in Darkhan. Many died repelling the Japanese invasion of 1939.

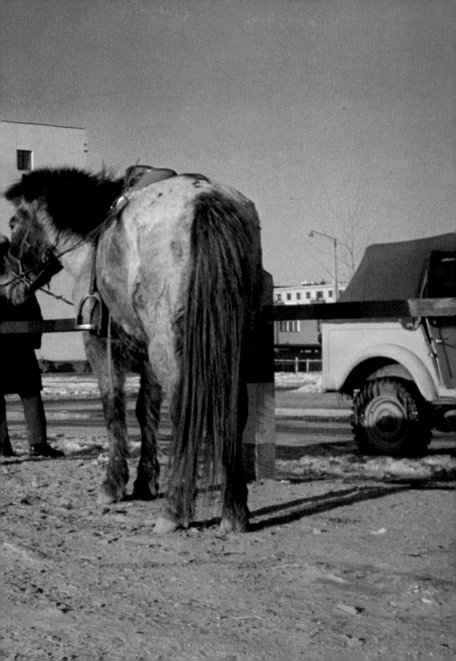

55. *A new department* store just opened in Darkhan; the signs in the foreground exhort the people to continue to help build social- ism.

56-57. *An oil refinery* has been constructed at Dzunbayan, near Sain Shand in the Gobi Desert, which scientists say has great untapped oil resources.

58. *A Russian soldier* from Irkutsk helps build a housing project in Darkhan; Russians not only ease the Mongol labor shortage but further cement Soviet-Mongol relations.

59-60. *Horses* are said to outnumber people in Mongolia by two to one. Most of the horses are small, rugged animals that look rather like ponies but that have tremendous stamina. Both horses and camels grow thick hair in the winter months to protect them against the bitter cold. The camels are carrying forage for livestock.

61. *An old man* with his grand-
children in front of their simple
wooden house in a remote region of
northern Mongolia; Mongol dress is
not very elegant but is eminently
practical.

62. *This couple* are the guards at a lev-▶
el railroad crossing on the trunk line
between Ulan Bator and Darkhan. The
walls of their house are partly covered
with hides for extra warmth.

63. *Collective farms* have imaginative names. This one is called Sukhe Bator's Way; others are Great Future, Initiative, Joyful Labor, Upsurge, and Marvelous.

64-66. *Mongolian scenes*: above, a pair of horsemen on a grassy steppe in summertime; below left, a rugged hill formation that has a strong appeal to the Mongol eye; below right, the death of an animal in the vast steppe country, far less frequent now than in the more primitive past.